MELODIOUS DOUBLE-STOPS

(Mélodies en Doubles-Cordes)

For Violin

By

JOSEPHINE TROTT

G. SCHIRMER, *Inc.*

DISTRIBUTED BY

HAL•LEONARD®
CORPORATION

7777 W. BLUEMOUND RD. P.O. BOX 13819 MILWAUKEE, WI 53213

Melodious Double-Stops

BOOK TWO
(First Position)

Violin

by Josephine Trott

* + Pizzicato with the left hand.

pizz.
l.h.

pizz.

Vigoroso

8

f

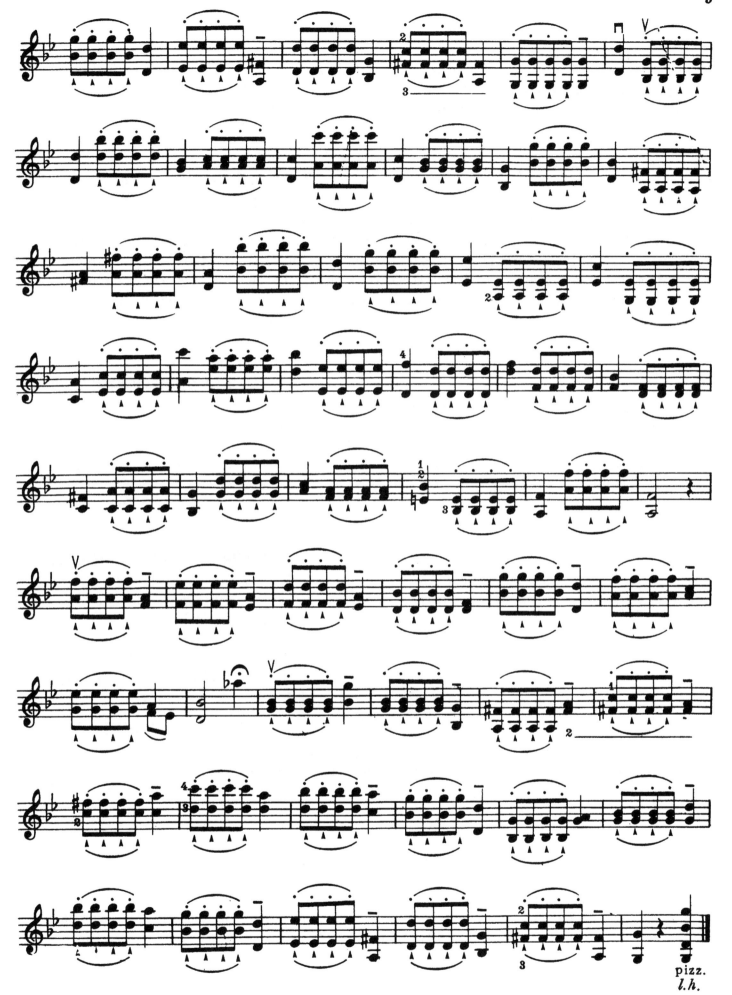

pizz.
l.h.

12

Espressivo

stay in 1st Pos.

rit. - - -

a tempo

p

harm.   harm.   harm.

Leggero

20

(lift bow with wrist)

lift bow

Lamentoso

23

28

ricochet